Yorkshire CURIOSITIES

W.R. Mitchell

DALESMAN

Dalesman Publishing Company
Stable Courtyard, Broughton Hall,
Skipton, North Yorkshire BD 23 3AE

First Published 1994
Copyright Dalesman Publishing

Compiled by **W.R. Mitchell**

Front cover: **Ripon Market Bell Man**
by **Clifford Robinson**

Back cover: **The Sphinx Watchman of Burnsall Fell**
by **Colin Raw**

A British Library Cataloguing in Publication
record is available for this book

ISBN 1 85568 079 3

All rights reserved. This book must not be circulated in any form of binding or cover other than that in which it is published and without similar condition of this being imposed on the subsequent purchaser. No part of this publication may be reproduced, stored on a retrieval system or transmitted in any form, or by any means, electronic, mechanical, photocopying, recording or otherwise, without either prior permission in writing from the publisher or a licence permitting restricted copying. In the United Kingdom such licences are issued by the Copyright Licensing Agency, 90 Tottenham Court Road, London W1P 9HE.

Contents

Introduction	5
1. Ancient Days	7
2. The Natural Way	16
3. Living History	23
4. Off to Church!	32
5. Some Yorkshire Follies	41
6. Storied Stones	48
7. Fabulous Dishes	52
8. Things that go Bump ...	59
9. At Random	64
Index	84
List of Illustrations	86

Brimham Rocks   The Dancing Bear   Bill Yates 1988

Introduction

Who'd Hev Thowt It?

The object of this book is to make you gasp with astonishment at intervals of a few minutes as you are introduced to some of the unusual objects and customs of Yorkshire, as recorded over a span of 50 years by readers of *The Dalesman*.

Your first gasp might be on hearing of a monument to some rock from outer space which embedded itself on the Yorkshire Wolds. Ivan Broadhead reported (1966) on a monument to "one of the most extraordinary phenomena of nature ever observed in this or any other part of the world." An inscription on a stone panel sandwiched between two trees in the middle of a field near Wold Newton noted that here, at about 3pm on December 13th, 1795, fell a 56lb meteorite.

At about that time, as editor of *The Dalesman*, I organised a competition for "Yorkshire Curiosities". The entries included a tinder box in a chest at the Merchant Adventurers' Hall in York, an obelisk at Darfield commemorating 189 men and boys killed in the Lundhill Colliery explosion of 1852, and an inscribed stone - "Do no Murder" - set in a hedgerow at Fingall, lower Wensleydale.

Included in this book are "curiosities" from the real Yorkshire - that which existed prior to the "mucking about" of county borders, and old loyalties, by the Boundary Commission in 1974. It is a big and varied county which defies generalisation.

Among the curiosities, from that same period, I might include the Yorkshire coat-of-arms, featuring a flea, a fly, a magpie and a bacon flitch. The flea is said to represent shrewdness and the fly hospitality. A magpie is linked with superstition, and a flitch of bacon is "never any good until it is hung - and so, by gum, is a Yorkshireman!"

Most of the curiosities mentioned in this book take a tangible form and range from a silver arrow (competed for in a competition which began at Scorton, near Richmond) to one of the great natural curiosities - Gaping Gill, the pothole on the flanks of Ingleborough, the main chamber of which has the appearance and proportions of a cathedral.

Included are follies like the Druid's Temple near Masham, enormous gooseberries which are judged at an annual show at Egton Bridge, in Eskdale, and the Cottingley Fairies, which convinced none other than Conan Doyle but turned out to be spurious. We might have known that for any Pennines fairies would quickly have their wings bedraggled by wind and rain and their ballet frocks spattered with mud.

W. R. MITCHELL

YOUNG RALPH CROSS
NEAR BLAKEY RIGG.

The church at Upleatham, near Saltburn, claimed to be the smallest church in the county by Clifford Robinson.

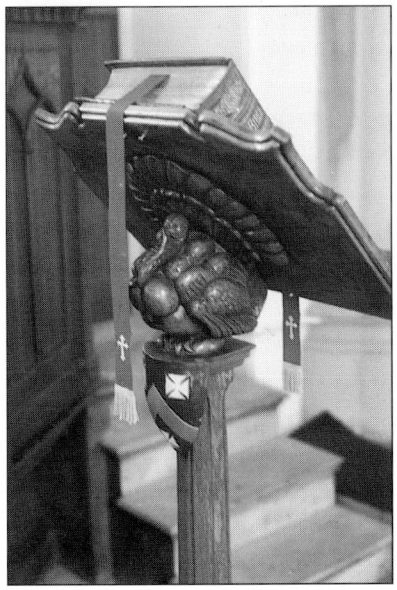

The Druid's Temple near Masham. Photographer not known.

Left, the Turkey Lectern at Boynton in the Wolds by W.R. Mitchell.

Chapter 1
Ancient Days

Broad Acres

Our pre-1974 Yorkshire, which is the one which matters, had close on four million acres (as many as there are letters in the Bible) and some five million people.

Devil's Arrows

The market town of Boroughbridge is situated on the south side of the river Ure, just upstream from its confluence with the Swale. There has been an important river crossing on the main north-south road in the vicinity since prehistoric times. For 2,000 years a settlement has here guarded that river crossing.

Half-a-mile to the west of Boroughbridge market-place stands three monoliths known as the Devil's Arrows. In the time of the 16th century historian, Leland, there were four: one has since disappeared, reputedly to form part of a bridge over the Tutt Beck.

Many theories have been suggested as to the stones' origin, but the one most commonly accepted is that they formed part of an enormous henge monument, or stone circle. Several such remains have been identified in the area, though the Devil's Arrows are by far the largest in scale.

Jane Hatcher (1974)

Rudston's Magical Monolith

Legend says that the Devil, enraged by the good people of Rudston, hurled a stone spear to smite them as they went to worship at the Church of All Saints. But by divine intervention, the javelin swerved, missing the church by a mere 12ft and burying half its length in the ground. There it remains to this day.

In truth, nobody really knows how the prehistoric monolith which dominates Rudston Churchyard came to be there. The Wolds village lies about five miles from Bridlington. In ancient times, it appears to have been a centre of activity as the area is dotted with tumuli, barrows and ancient dykes.

The monolith, almost 26ft high, is the tallest standing stone in Britain. It is made of gritstone, of which the nearest source is some ten miles distant. Its overall size and weight are not known. Experts believe that a two foot section may have broken off the top. Studies carried out in the 18th century by Sir William Strickland estimated that the stone might extend as far below the ground as it extends into the air.

It seems likely that, in an attempt to convert Rudston Monolith into a Christian symbol, a cross-member was at one time added, providing Rudston with its name, "rood" being Old English for cross and "stan" for stone.

Robin Richards (1994)

Cups and Rings

Balanced on a ridge, half a mile east of the Cow and Calf rocks above Ilkley, rests the Pancake Rock. Given the right conditions, hang-gliding enthusiasts launch themselves from the bracken slopes nearby.

This is a place of rock and air, wind and open space - and mystery. The upper surfaces of Pancake Rock are carved with shallow cups. This is a cup and ring stone, inscribed by prehistoric man, probably with an antler tip, nearly 4,000 years ago. Bronze Age man stood on this rock looking out across Wharfedale.

Over the years, many people walking these moors will have seen some of the carved rocks but few will know there are over 250 examples of this Bronze Age art within a few square miles of Rombald's Moor. Many hours walking, looking, measuring and mapping by local archaeologists have revealed and recorded one of the largest concentrations of prehistoric rock art in the British Isles.

Hollow cups, dots, groups of dots, circles open and closed, grooves down from the cups, lines joining, lines extending, curved ladders joining rings inside rings, and a swastika with a hooked tail - what kind of message do they convey? Can we translate it? Who can provide the clues?

For over 100 years, antiquarians and archaeologists have speculated on the meaning of these carvings. Naturally each age sees and interprets these signs through its own concerns... The past stands before us, revealed but still mysterious.

Derek Hyatt (1986)

Danes Dyke

There's a vagueness about the story of Danes Dyke at Flamborough Head. Trees hide the main feature - the dyke which is said to be man-made at the northern end and, in the south, is formed by a natural ravine gouged out by thundering meltwater from the icefields towards the end of the Pleistocene period.

I've heard some strange theories extolled about the Danes Dyke. One man was quite sure it was the track of a comet that had come to earth. Another fancied that the width of the Dyke was dictated by the average bowshot. If so, the average bowman was puny indeed.

About 2,000 years ago, the Dyke appears to have become a major defensive earthwork. Who made it so, we do not known, but it is much older than the immigrant Danes who may, indeed, have had their name attached to it when they carried out some repairs.

Pat Wilson, manager at Manor Farm, mentioned that at the Danes Dyke there appears to be an abrupt transition between chalk and boulder clay. The Dyke, quiet and secluded, offering woodland and shelter in a flat, gale-swept area, is highly attractive to migratory birds.

In October and November, it is not unusual to see as many as 1,000 goldcrests, freshly arrived after a long sea crossing, in the bushes at the bottom end of the Dyke.

W. R. Mitchell (1984)

The Corpse Way

Crossing Kisdon Hill, between Keld and Muker, then fording the Swale and continuing up Iveletside, high up along the north slope of Swaledale, runs an ancient track which is now known as The Corpse Way. It was used by funeral parties when they carried their dead from the dalehead to a final resting place at the parish church of Grinton.

Dr Whitaker, writing 150 years ago, said that "before interments began to take place at Muker, the bodies of the dead were conveyed for burial upon men's shoulders upwards of 12 miles to the parish church, not in coffins, but in crude wicker baskets.

Funerals from West Stonesdale, Frith, Smithyholme and Ravenseat kept to the left bank of the Swale and joined the Way at Calvert Houses. Two pall-bearers were supplied from each of these hamlets in addition to the family bearers, so that the carrying could be done in relays.

Before the procession began, watch was kept over the body by each of the relatives in turn. Special biscuits and wine were handed over the wicker-coffin to the guests as they arrived. All the neighbours were "bidden" by personal calls, and sometimes as many as 200 would attend the service.

When a shepherd died, a fleece of wool was placed in his coffin. His occupation could thus be proved on Judgement Day, so that his irregular attendance at church would be forgiven.

While the journey lasted, the funeral guests lived at the expense of the bereaved. At intervals along the route, the body was laid upon stone slats or resting-stones, while the cortege halted for a while.

Travelling from the head of Swaledale to Grinton would take at least two days, depending on the state of the weather. Just above the village of Feetham are the ruined foundations of a building known as the "dead house", where the wicker coffins were left in safety while the procession slipped down to what is now the *Punch Bowl*, to rest and refresh themselves.

Two funeral parties using the wayside mortuary at the same time realised, only after the burial service had taken place, and when the effects of the "refreshment" had worn off, that the bodies had been interred in the wrong graves.

Edmund Cooper (1963)

Moorland Crosses

Sentinels of lonely places, rubbing posts for hardy moorland sheep and objects of passing interest to the hiker, are the old grey-stoned crosses of the North York Moors.

Two crosses - Ralph Cross East and Ralph Cross West - stand near Westerdale. The East cross is interesting because of a pleasing custom of leaving a coin in the cup-like depression on the head of the cross to assist the more needy wayfarer who passes that way.

A quaint saying in the district is that if the East cross and White Cross (known locally as Fat Betty), which stands nearby, happen to meet - there will be a wedding.

Norman Giddins (1951)

Bridestones

The mushroom-shaped Bridestones straddle a 800ft high ridge above Dovedale and Staindale, backed by the North York Moors. A fanciful story tells of a newly-married couple who spent the first night here, hence the name.

Geologists relate that about 60,000 years ago, erosion on the lower slopes of the ridge began to expose cliffs composed of Jurassic sandstones. These are alternately siliceous (which is relatively strong) and calcareous (much weaker). Not only was a cliff formed, but further erosion made inroads into the cliff, creating buttresses and then isolated outcrops.

A grassed-over hummock on the ridge will, in due course, be exposed to wind, rain and frost and become an outcrop of naked rock. Given a few more thousand years of erosion, a Bridestone would be formed. Nature is never still, for the process of erosion would lead to it being gradually washed away as particles of sand, to settle in the valley far below.

W. R. Mitchell (1988)

Cow and Calf Rocks

These two enormous pieces of gritstone are frequently among the pictures selected for calendars. They dominate the road which climbs out of Ilkley and from them are extensive views of Wharfedale.

The Bull, third and largest rock in the Ilkley Moor group, stood much nearer to the road and on its side its name was cut out in enormous letters.

Some years prior to 1860, a dispute arose between the quarry contractors and the Lord of the Manor regarding the right of the former to break up the "Bull" rock for building purposes. The case went in favour of the quarry contractors.

So the rock was broken up and the fragments of stone used in building the Crescent Hotel, which was opened in 1860.

Edmund Bogg

Civic Arms

Every Yorkshireman will know that the White Rose is the emblem of the House of York. Oddly enough, it does not appear in the bearings of the City of York. The rose was the emblem of the House of York before the Wars of the Roses but our three Ridings include three York roses in a band, known as the chief, across the top of the shield.

One reason for the City of York omitting our county emblem may be due to the fact that it proudly boasts five gold lions. The lion, which is usually most imaginative in design due to artists' licence, is of course a Royal emblem and has been so since the time of Richard I.

York is one of our oldest cities. It is said that on Christmas Day, 1251, King Henry III visited York to confer a knighthood on Alexander, the youthful monarch of the Scots. This took place in the Archbishop's palace near the Minster and, according to the original order, we know that the Queen was dressed in a violet-coloured brocade heraldically adorned with three leopards (or lions) on the front of her dress.

The Mayor of York was present, his banner bearing "The Five Lions of York". A curious fact about this is an unsupported fable that the insignia of the five lions upon a shield was granted by William the Conqueror in commemoration of five brave defenders of the City of York when besieged and destroyed by his soldiers.

When the design was produced there was a profound respect for the ensign of St George, adopted as the main charge on the shield. No doubt the symbol of the lions or leopards was intended to convey a power of strength to the opposing soldiers.

The shield is crested with a Cap of Maintenance - or Cap of Dignity - which along with the sword and mace form the emblems of the Lord Mayor's authority.

Chapter 2

The Natural Way

Yorkshire, a country within a county, is well-endowed with natural features, from a petrifying well (where a rock face has to be scraped every six weeks to prevent it from becoming top heavy) to a subterranean chamber which is the size of a cathedral.

A Petrifying Well

Knaresborough's Dropping Well has been nationally famous since medieval times. Leland referred to it in his tour of England and Wales in the 1520s, while the first opening to the public is recorded as having taken place a century later. Serious rock falls occurred in 1816 and 1821.

The petrifying action of the water has been found by analysis to be due to a preponderance of lime and sulphates as well as smaller quantities of chlorides and magnesium. Its rate of flow remains absolutely constant at 20 gallons a minute.

The Dropping Well, which of course is really a cliff and not a well at all in the normally accepted sense of the term, is unique in Britain, although a more conventional well into which articles are lowered for petrification exists at Matlock.

The owner told me: "We get about half-a-dozen suitable objects given each year, although of course we receive hundreds of odd socks and gloves. The kind of items that are suitable are sponges, parasols, stuffed animals and birds, teddy bears and children's clothes - in fact anything porous."

The period of petrification varies according to size. A sponge takes as little as six weeks. But a teddy bear for instance requires what may be termed 18 dripping months - an actual period of three years, as all objects have to be taken down at the end of each season to prevent frost damage.

David Joy (1970)

Ebbing and Flowing

Giggleswick's patron saint, Alkelda (note the *-keld*, which means spring), may be none other than a Christianisation of an old deity of what became known as the holy well.

The most famous well in the district lies beside the road at the bottom of Buckhaw Brow. Known as the Ebbing and Flowing Well, its special properties have been commented on for centuries. At times of moderate rainfall, water in a stone trough may suddenly flow away. The trough then re-fills.

The action is said to be caused by a double syphon in the limestone within Giggleswick Scar. Two American visitors of 1840, who wished to discover the secret behind the well, hired workmen to take the well to pieces and then replace it. In the process they are said to have replaced at the base of the well, face downwards, an inscribed stone which gives a mystical explanation of the phenomenon.

It ascribes it to a miracle performed long ago by a priest who wanted to show an evil-doer the wickedness of his ways. According to a paper owned by the Pig Yard Club, the inscription reads: "Ye water dyd run yn even course botte Prioure Richard Moone bie ye power from above dyd mak it to rise and to fall yn in a most curious manner so that he (the evil-doer) dyd afterwards paie his tithes and dyd forsake hys evylie waies."

One of the most informed men was the Rev George Brown, of Settle. He walked to the well every day in 1899, sometimes arriving at 5am, and each time he spent over an hour studying its conduct. Several times, chiefly in June, he saw the silver cord which is caused by an air current passing through the water.

W. R. Mitchell (1964)

Gagates and Snakestones

On a certain stretch of the Yorkshire coast, the characteristic holidaymaker is not of the comic postcard type, but a crouched or stooping figure, whose face is turned towards neither sun nor sea, but bent to the rocks and shingle on the beach or to the debris below a cliff. This holidaymaker is looking for jet or fossils.

The best time to search for jet - "gagates" to the Romans - is just after ebb tide with a nor'easter blowing round the points and across the scars, piling up weed and debris on the shingle and among the creeks. Being light in weight, small pieces of jet lodge on the surface. It is then that three or four lads will be seen combing the beach and cannily filling plastic bags. Clean, hard jet of the Whitby sort sells for up to £4 per pound weight at a lapidary's.

Beginners may find jet difficult to distinguish from similar worn pieces of shale or coal. The test is to rub your piece on a dry sandstone boulder. Shale or slate leave a white mark, coal a black, but jet - wood from ancestors of the Monkey Puzzle tree, flattened and fossilised under the mud of the sea bed - leaves a pale brown mark. It also stays shiny when dry and is highly electric under friction.

Seams found in strata above those of ironstone and below those of alum, once extensively mined at Boulby, vary from one to six inches in width. Miners from Staithes, Runswick, Hinderwell, Mulgrave, Kettleness and Sandsend supplied a trade, centred on Whitby, which then employed nearly 1,500 workers.

Scores of jet workshops turned out beads, necklaces, crosses, brooches, pendants, lockets and bonnet ornaments, carved in a material which Queen Victoria's period of mourning had made high fashion. While the boom lasted, craftsmen could earn £3-4 a week.

"Snakestones" were also offered for sale a century ago, in places where there were layers of oolite strata, such as Scarborough, Whitby and, at the other end of the belt, Lyme Regis and Weymouth, "where people came with a little scientific taste, more leisure and most money.".

Whitby snakestones are explained in Sir Walter Scott's notes to *Marmion*. Coils of stone, "the reliques of the snakes which infested the precincts of the convent and were, at the Abbess's (St Hilda's) prayer, not only beheaded but petrified, are still found about the rocks and are termed by Protestant fossilists Ammonitae.

About 200 species of ammonite occur in layers and are to be found in nodules, either loose or embedded in the cliff face. Broken open with a geologist's hammer, they reveal "the coiled up ringed shell wonderfully resembling a snake and still more wonderfully, when they put a 'head' on with eyes," as sellers, keeping alive the legend.

Huge ammonites and the first bones of Time," mentioned as garden ornaments by Tennyson, are not so thick on the ground as they were even five years ago. Collectors, students, overseas visitors and dealers have seen to that.

Charles Marsden (1981)

The Gypsey Race

This straggling stream, steeped in legend and tradition, carves its way through East Riding farmland and village until it reaches the sea at Bridlington.

In the summer months, the Race is usually reduced to a trickle. But in the winter, swollen by the rains and snows, it rushes through the countryside like a torrent and has on occasions flooded some of the villages in its path.

Tradition has it that the Race was running before the Great Plague struck England in 1665, but many people say that the waters did not begin to move until much later. It was recorded as running in 1795, the year a meteor hurtled to the ground at Wold Newton.

Some say the name of the watercourse comes from the Greek word, *gupos*, meaning chalk. Others claim it originated from the gipsy people in the fact that it wanders. The most likely solution, however, is that it comes from the Norse term, *gypa*, which means gushing stream or geyser.

There was a time when the young people of Burton Fleming went out to "meet the Gypsey", a custom which shows an instance of water worship in the olden days. The people went out to meet and praise the spirit whose power caused the stream to flow.

Because the Gipsey Race suddenly appears and disappears through the effect of underground springs, it was given the title "Woe Waters":

> *The Gypsey I trow is my ancient name,*
> *My Sponsors Northmen like gold,*

Oh, it is a name of most eerie fame,
I'm the woe waters of the Wold.

Villagers thought the advent of the waters foretold famine or hard times. Today, those stories are unbelievable, but tales of the Gypsey Race form a fascinating and important link with days gone by.

Mary Fowler (1966)

Scarborough's Hidden Wells

The calendar read 1626, and this particular year was to prove the making of a tiny Yorkshire fishing village named Scarborough. A certain Mrs Farrow wandered about the village feeling thoroughly out of sorts and full of all the aches and pains that were most prevalent and popular in those days.

She paused to rest beside a spring which bubbled up rusty coloured water. She was so tired and thirsty that she took her life and her health in her hands and drank some of the revolting looking fluid. Then she took of her shoes and stockings and bathed her aching feet.

Suddenly, Mrs Farrow felt refreshed and slightly eased of her aches and pains. She stared at the waters with speculative eyes and decided on the spot that anything which tasted so acrid, and looked so vile, must be good for the health in some way or other.

Her medico, Dr Whittle, agreed with his valuable and well-off patient that there might be something medicinally valuable in the spring waters. He also decided, secretly to himself this time, that there might be a lot in it financially as well, with a windbag like the aching Mrs Farrow to go the rounds telling her story to other achers.

He began to prescribe the waters to his other patients and

also prescribed, as a sideline, the drinking of 25 gallons of sea water, taken a pint at a time, over a period. A good bath would have cleaned the clogged-up pores of his sufferers, but it would not have been good manners to put this thought into words. Instead, he took the opportunity of suggesting that they might all try total submersion in the sea itself.

From that day onwards, Scarborough was made. The wells were developed and a white marble staircase and other structures were built round the wells. Then, in 1875, a bandstand was constructed on top of the wells. An underground pump room was developed, beautified with tables and chairs and with ferns and flowers and a bar. Fireplace-like surrounds were made round the north and south wells, as they came to be called.

The pump rooms were a tremendous success at the time, but by 1909 the novelty seemed to have worn off. The pump room was closed down until 1925, when it was once more revived and became a great attraction with visitors. Then, in 1932, the pump room was altered and used for a few years, being then closed down once more.

Twenty years afterwards, two workmen crawled down through a manhole and found the old wells standing there in a sad state of repair in their circular home. It was intended to commercialise the waters and sell them in bottles. Unfortunately, the demand for the waters was not sufficient to make the venture a success.

Now the pump room is closed, waiting for some future generation to discover it anew and ponder over its purpose.

D. M. Priestley (1966)

Inside Ripon Cathedral.

Below Morris dancing at Masham Sheep Show by W.R. Mitchell.

Wainhouse Tower in the Vale of Calder by J. Boothroyd.

Chapter 3

Living History

The past impinges on the present, as in much blowing of horns, the planting of a hedge in the harbour at Whitby - and the burning of the effigy of a sheep-stealer in Wensleydale.

Seven Hornblasts at Ripon

At Bainbridge, in the upper valley of the Ure, a farmer blows the Forest Horn on winter evenings. Dalesfolk do not like a lot of frills to life, and the hornblower wears no special clothes. Local people do insist upon punctuality, which is why he has never been able to listen to the nine o'clock news.

At Ripon-on-the-Skell, a tributary of the Ure, the even more famous Wakeman's Horn is blown nightly, throughout the year. Ripon folk are proud of their long history. They deck their hornblower in a buff coat with scarlet cuffs and collar. The brass buttons have the Corporation insignia featured in relief.

Bainbridge uses a horn from an African buffalo, and it is not the original horn. There is talk of the custom going back to the days when a Roman fort stood in the village. Ripon has a similar horn, though it is doubtful if it came from the same buffalo. Ripon's hornblowing history is well-documented; the custom originated in the ninth century, when the Wakeman was responsible for the safety of the household goods and property of the Ripon people.

Hornblowing is a specialist occupation which tends to run in families. Somewhere along the line you discover an association with a Yorkshire brass band. The Hawleys of Ripon served in the local band and benefit from it when they took up animal, as opposed to mineral, hornblowing.

The horn is blown at 9pm. Cyril Hawley told me about the custom: "I have never missed the appointment in the market place and, to our knowledge, the custom has been carried on unbroken, every night, since the year 886." He leaves home at about 8.40pm, and apart from his distinctive coat he wears a beaver tricorn.

The outfit appeals to visitors. In between hornblasts it is possible to hear the clicking of camera shutters. The horn is semi-circular, totalling about three feet in length, and it has been used since 1865. It is blown seven times each evening - four times in the market square (once at each corner of the 90ft high market cross) and three times outside the Mayor's home, which must be visited before midnight.

Ripon's horn produces a "long bellowing sound." It has been heard well over a mile from the market cross when helped along by the wind.

W. R. Mitchell (1967)

The Horngarth

A vigorous shout, "Out on ye: Out on ye!" followed three thin blasts on a cow horn. It was the Eve of Ascension Day at Whitby, where for over 800 years the Ceremony of the Penny Hedging or Horngarth has been faithfully enacted.

Legend maintains that it all began in the reign of Henry II, when the Lord of Ugglebarney, a small settlement outside the town, thrilled to the chase. The noble lord rented land originally bestowed on St Hilda, Foundress of the Abbey, by King Oswin. This land, and the hunting rights which accompanied it, were retained by succeeding abbots, and all prerogatives were jealously guarded.

On one occasion, in the heat of the chase, the lord and his two companions wounded a boar. The terrified animal took refuge in the cell of a monk from the abbey, who himself had sought solitude in a cave within the woods of Eskdale. The holy man is said to have barred the door to the huntsmen, whereupon they, in their excitement and frustration, ran a boar stave through the body of the hermit.

On his deathbed, the monk demanded that a penance should be meted out to the three lords and their descendants. On the Eve of Ascension Day each year in perpetua, an Officer of the Abbey should await descendants of the said William de Bruce at sunrising. The Abbot's representative was instructed to blow his horn to announce his whereabouts in the forest near the little village of Sandsend.

The penitents were then to cut with "a penny knife" a specified number of hazel boughs, "ten stakes, ten Stout Stowers, and ten Yedders", which they were to bear on their backs into the town of Whitby, arriving there at nine in the morning. The stakes were to be driven into the shore on a receding tide, "at the Brim of the Water", each stake a yard from the next.

Should the families of the said Walter de Bruce and his friends... fail to perform this rite - or if the hedge they constructed was so insubstantial that it did not withstand three tides - they were to "forfeit all their lands to the Abbot and his successors".

Another and more credible version of the ancient custom attributes a more useful purpose to the erection of the hedge, which on hunting days was to trap such animals as swam the river when the herds were driven from the forests towards the town.

It is unlikely that posterity will ever know the truth of the matter, but to this day the good citizens of Whitby observe the Ceremony of Planting the Penny Hedge.

M. Nixon (1983)

Scorton Arrow

We in Yorkshire claim that Robin Hood was a native of Wakefield who way-laid his rich victims in the Forest of Barnsdale. At Canon Hall, near Barnsley, I was once shown a longbow said to have been owned by Little John, one of Robin's "merry men".

The longbow, terror-weapon of medieval battles, is still in action. Some of the arrows used are traditional, having feathers from the grey goose as fledglings, or stabilisers, but technology has enhanced even this ancient sport. The old longbow was made of Spanish yew; the modern bow, with its man-made materials and spiky embellishments, weighs less than a third of that of yore.

The Scorton Silver Arrow, first competed for in 1673, takes its name from a small village near Richmond. There is no older archery competition in the land, the first Scorton event taking place three years before the formation of the Queen's Bodyguard for Scotland. Shooting for this prized arrow and other silver prizes is still governed by 17th century rules.

The story of the arrow is complex but folklore associates it with the second son of the local squire. As put to me by an official, he was "caught in the wrong bed with a serving wench." The family banished him.

Sir Henry Calverley heard the story, possibly as an item of dinner table gossip, and he knew that the banished man had a silver arrow he had won at Oxford. It was the traditional prize given for archery contests in those days. Calverley acquired the arrow and put it up for annual competition. It would be given to the first man to strike gold.

He himself won it on the first occasion. Developments in the construction and accuracy of bows led to a three-inch diameter black zone being placed on the gold to make it more difficult. In due course, it was reduced to two inches.

A silver spoon is awarded to the worst shot at the end of the day. It is related that in the 18th century it was won by a man who had a large family. The children developed a habit of not going to bed at night until they had had their gruel, using the spoon for this meal.

Over the years, seven little sets of teeth wore away the end of the spoon to such an extent that the man who had won it as a prize had to get the local silversmith to bind it in silver. Inscribed on the back in Latin are words which are translated as: "Withhold your laughter, friends."

W. R. Mitchell (1992)

Derby Day at Kiplingcotes

It may lack the glamour of the Ebor and the prestige of the Leger but that won't worry the hardy souls who gather for what will, in all probability, be another chilly Kiplingcotes Derby.

There is a certain bloody-minded pride in staging the world's oldest endowed horse race and they don't let a drop of rain, a few feet of snow or even an absence of runners stop them holding the evening each third Thursday in March.

Locals and experts disagree over its history. The winning post carries the date 1519, which tradition dictates was the first running, but the first official evidence of a race at Kibling Coates, as it was then called, dates back to 1555, when it is mentioned in court evidence.

Others, including Major Fairfax-Blakeborough, give 1619 as the date while in 1746 the *Newcastle Chronicle* reported a meeting that included several races and a football match.

Whatever its infancy, there is no dispute that the race has developed some very strange ways on its way to maturity, some so obscure that they might have been devised especially for the benefit of sports trivialists.

The runners weigh in at the finish before going four miles to the start. The jockeys have to meet the ten stone minimum, minus their saddles, and carry any extra weight on their bodies instead. The second-placed rider usually gets a bigger prize than the winner.

Once the runners have gathered at the starting post, near the old Kiplingcotes station, it is a fast, gruelling run over muddy fields and tracks back to the finish near Middleton-on-the-Wold. In good conditions, the winner can cover the course in about ten minutes, but if winter stays late on the Wolds, deep snow can slow down horses dramatically.

In 1947, conditions were so bad no entries were received. So a local farmer, Fred Stephenson, walked his horse over the course to ensure the tradition remained unbroken. His "winning" time for the (literally) one-horse race was 1 hour 20 minutes.

Terry Fletcher (1994)

Nine Tailors Make a Man

Years ago, I was staying in Middleham and one morning the church bell began to ring at an unusual time. My hostess raised her finger for silence, and after the first few peals, a single bell rang out. She counted one to nine, and then murmured: "It's a man."

Another peal, and again the single bell; it continued to ring and we counted to the 1970s, and then she said: "Eh! it mun be ould Kit as had flitten, he's been ailing aff and on fur lang eneaf. Ah wonder when the side-ing will be?" Then the bells continued the "passing".

She then explained to me that the first peal denoted a death; the nine denoted a "man" (three would denote a woman), the number which followed gave the age, so that everyone within the sound of the bell would give a shrewd guess as to who had passed on.

The "passing bell" which followed varied according to the spirit of the relatives; generous folk gave a long "passing"; stingy ones gave a short one; for the sexton was paid by them according to the length of time. The reason for the bell was to scare off evil spirits and to give the soul of the departed a fair chance of gaining the port of heaven before the evil spirits could catch it.

The single bell to denote the age is called a "teller", which by some means has been mis-spelt "tailor"; the saying therefore should be "nine tellers mean a man" and is no discredit to the occupation of a tailor.

P. V. Oliver (1939)

Burning of Bartle

The ancient custom of the Burning of Bartle at West Witton in Wensleydale takes place on the evening of St Bartholomew, which is towards the end of August. The origin of the custom is obscure. I heard the most likely explanation from the third generation of village blacksmiths who said that this story had been handed down from his grandfather.

The Forest of Wensleydale once stretched from east of Middleham to west of West Witton, including Penhill, immediately south of the village. Long before the days of village constables, a vagabond used to raid the forest and steal some swine belonging to the villagers. Eventually they took the only safe course open to them and they joined together in rounding him up.

They chased him down the slopes of the fellside towards the village. According to the doggerel shouted by the Chief Executioner, who helps to carry an effigy of Bartle from the top of the village in the darkness on St Bartholomew's Day, it seems almost certain that, in the chase, Bartle had his neck broken before he was finally committed to the flames, in Grassgill Lane.

At this spot each year the ceremony concludes by burning the effigy at the stake, but the man who has made that effigy for many years takes care to first remove certain oddments, including an electric battery which has provided light for his eyes.

The doggerel relates:

> *At Penhill crags he tore his rags,*
> *At Hunter's Thorn he blew his horn,*
> *At Capplebank Stee (stile) he brak his knee,*
> *At Griskill (Grassgill) beck he brak his neck,*
> *At Waddam's End he couldn't fend,*
> *At Griskill End will be his end.*

One old inhabitant had the custom linked with the Penhill Giant, who was said to have been buried in a grave on the West Witton side of Penhill. The grave is large enough to hold ten normal men.

R. B. Fawcett (1966)

Chapter 4

Off to Church!

Our Yorkshire churches are, apart from their continuing mission, the repository of many curious objects from past ages. Quite apart from places of worship used today are the remains of great abbeys and priories.

Green Man Mystery

The austerity of the Cistercians of Fountains Abbey did not permit much in the way of decorative sculpture; and probably the majority of visitors to the Abbey remain unaware that there are any examples at all.

Of the few which have been tolerated, the most striking and surprising is on the outside of the building, at the apex of one of the tall arched windows of the Chapel of the Nine Altars - the stone head of a man, prominent because it is the only piece of decoration on the whole of an external wall.

Closer inspection will reveal that it is a strange man, indeed, for branches grow out of his mouth, twining upwards and downwards to frame the face with leaves. He is, in fact, the Green Man, well-known as an inn sign as well as a feature of church decoration.

His origins are obscure. His characteristic is the foliage, commonly oak or vine, which grows from his mouth and frequently his nostrils and eyebrows, sometimes so sparsely that the features are clearly revealed, sometimes so luxuriantly that the leaves form a mask through which the eyes peep.

The Fountains Green Man, one of the later in date, from

the 15th century, is of a more sympathetic type than some. In nearby Ripon Cathedral, a corbel on the outside of the building incorporates a 13th century Green Man of the more menacing kind.

The identity of the Green Man remains a mystery, however. He is almost certainly the same character who, as "Jack in the Green", figured in ceremonial occasions in the Middle Ages. He wore a costume which covered him completely with leaves, as some inn signs still show; and played the role of the fool or jester, dancing ahead of the procession or even throwing fireworks to force back the spectators.

At the May Day celebration, he took a prominent part in the dancing and fooling, only to have his costume formally burned at the end of the day with the same expressions of hostility and derision later associated with Guy Fawkes.

This takes us even further back in our search for his origins, to very ancient pagan, possibly Druidic, rites concerned with Nature's cycle of decay and resurrection, when the costume of foliage had a human sacrifice inside it when it was burned.

A new Green Man was then forthwith nominated, with the dubious privilege of holding office until next year's flames. This represented the ending of one of the cycles of seasons, from which, phoenix-like, a new cycle of vegetation was reborn, along with a new Green Man.

When Abbot Darnton of Fountains Abbey, in 1483, needed to repair a window damaged by settling foundations, it was consequently in some respects strange that he should have incorporated the head of the pagan Green Man in the repairs.

He possibly thought of it as merely a folk symbol commonly used in church decoration at that time, which the inhabitants of the valley of the river Skell would immediately recognise from stories which they knew, without feeling it to be particularly anti-Christian.

Howard Strick (1978)

Swinnergill Kirk

A church with a waterfall for its door sounds like fantasy, and to reach Swinnergill Kirk demands a rough walk in the Kisdon district of upper Swaledale.

In a small valley leading down to the Swale, the Swinnergill falls over a ledge of rock, and behind a sheet of water is a cave. What better secret meeting place for those who adhered to the old faith during the Reformation could be desired? Traces of crude pictures and scriptural texts may still be traced on the walls and until recent date even the large block of stone which served as an altar remained.

The cave was also used as a refuge after a skirmish between dalesmen and a party of Scots during the 1745 rebellion. That Prince Charlie had adherents in North Yorkshire is without doubt and there is a tradition in the Birkbeck family that after the defeat of '45, two brothers -

James and George Birkbeck - wandered into Swaledale and settled at Melbecks.

They planted two Scotch fir trees as a sign that if any supporters of the Stuart cause were in need, they would be secretly and hospitably received at "the sign of the two firs".

M. H. Horn (1939)

The Pickering Frescoes

During the Middle Ages, the interiors of churches - especially the nave - were decorated with brightly coloured frescoes depicting Biblical stories. This seems to have had a two-fold object: to instruct as well as adorn.

Bridge to the inner ward
Pickering Castle

At the time of the Reformation, many of these frescoes were either destroyed or covered with plaster and were thus lost to sight for centuries. Those at Pickering were not discovered until the plaster covering them was removed during restoration in 1851.

They were painted during the years 1452-54. The visitor entering the church through the south door is faced by a portrait of St Christopher; other pictures are of St George and the Dragon, the crowning of the Virgin and the martyrdom of Saints John the Baptist, Thomas a Becket and Edmund. The latter picture is distinctly harrowing.

The pictures on the south wall of the nave are scenes from the life of St Catherine of Alexandria.

The Veronica Handkerchief

A picture of Jesus Christ hangs in Hutton Rudby church. To the casual observer, it would appear to be a sepia and white print of little interest.

On closer inspection, I found in very small print at the bottom of the picture something to the effect that if anyone looks very carefully at the closed eyes of the likeness, they will appear to open.

I duly concentrated on the closed eyes on the picture and found to my amazement that they did open - or so I thought. According to legend, it is a print depicting the features of the Veronica handkerchief. I do not know if a similar object can be seen elsewhere.

H. R. Miller (1966)

Pulpits and Pews

There are several Jacobean pulpits in Yorkshire. That in the church of St Cuthbert, Crayke, is dated 1637 and bears the inscription: "Show me thy waes, O Lord, and teach me thy paths". The pews in this church are of the same date.

Three-decker pulpits are uncommon but there are at least four in Yorkshire. The chapel-like church of St Laurence,

Aldfield, is dominated by a relatively massive three-decker, dated 1783. The lower deck is entered from the nave and was the seat of the sexton, one of whose duties as to say "Amen" at the appropriate times. The upper two decks, one for the conduct of the service and the other for the delivery of the sermon, are entered from the chancel.

There is a three-decker and a squire's parlour fitted with an open fireplace in the church of All Saints, Weston. The most ornate three-decker pulpit ever built is in the church of St Andrew, Slaidburn. Pevsner (1959) described it as "an uncommonly attractive stately three-decker of the c.18th."

Frith Stools

Three frith or frid stools are to be found in the north. The original design is probably best illustrated by the massive stone chair now lodged on the north side of the sanctuary of Beverley Minster.

Its stark simplicity will be, for some, its attraction. It is a Pre-Conquest stone chair, thought to have been used by the officer investigating pleas for sanctuary. (Macmahon, 1975).

Cyril Polson (1984)

The Devil's Knell

"Tolling the Devil's Knell" on Christmas Eve has been a custom at Dewsbury for about 600 years. Sir Thomas de Soothill, a local nobleman, suffered from fits of temper and during one such fit he murdered his servant boy. He hid the body in Forge Dam, a mill pond nearby.

When his temper had subsided, he realised the profound wickedness of his actions and became afraid for his soul. In a mistaken attempt to atone for his actions, he presented to Dewsbury Parish Church a 13cwt tenor bell, with instructions that it should be rung on Christmas Eve at a slow pace, as at a funeral, one toll for every year since Christ was born.

"Black Tom" has been rung every year since. The last stroke is exactly at midnight, after which the first Communion of Christmas is celebrated.

All Saints, now one of five churches within the Team Parish of Dewsbury, was in 1993 raised to minster status. Paulinus, a missionary who arrived in England from Rome in 623, to accompany Augustine on the conversion of the Saxons to Christianity, came to Northumbria with Queen Ethelberga upon her marriage to King Edwin in 627. Tradition has it that he preached and celebrated at Dewsbury.

Richard Middleton (Pennine Magazine, 1993)

Beverley's White Rabbit

St Mary's, at Beverley, was erected in no less than 15 stages, spread almost continuously over some 400 years. So it reveals, as few churches do, the whole panorama of English medieval architecture.

St Mary's began life round about 1120 as a chapel-of-ease to the minster, meaning that in all respects it was subject to the jurisdiction of the Chapter. Yet this church is one of the most absorbing parish churches in the land.

Those with a more than passing knowledge of St Mary's pause before a label-stop in St Michael's chapel. Here is a carving of a pilgrim rabbit, which - according to legend - was the inspiration for Lewis Carroll and the illustrator Tenniel and thus has gone round the world with the classic children's book, Alice Through the Looking Glass.

T.L.

A Turkey Lectern

Providing an unusual support for a lectern in the village church at Boynton, on the Wolds, is a carved turkey. It is actually a crest for a coat-of-arms, granted to one William Strickland for bringing the first turkeys to Britain from the New World early in the 16th century.

Strickland commanded one of Sebastian Cabot's ships in an expedition which sailed from Bristol. The convoy anchored off the American coast, and on leading a party ashore to forage for food Strickland found that the natives had some semi-domesticated turkeys. Intrigued by them, he took some back to Britain, where the turkey became the traditional Christmas dish.

Strickland applied for a crest for a coat-of-arms, and Clarenceux, King of Arms, granted him in 1550 the crest he requested: "A turkey in its proper pride, beaked, membered, sable coated and wattled gules." Strickland died in 1598. He is still well remembered through the turkey-lectern.

Eric Harris (1959)

A Leeds Organ

The Schulze Organ at St Bartholomew's Church, Armley, Leeds, is noted for the exceptional beauty and majesty of its tones.

The organ has had a strange history, being built and voiced not for any church but as a concert instrument in a large wooden "organ house" capable of seating some 800, in the grounds of The Towers, Meanwood, Leeds. Here it was played by Mrs Kennedy, wife of Thomas Stuart Kennedy, an engineer and alpinist, who was also a music-lover and for whom the neo-Gothic mansion with its exotic chimneys had just been built to the design of Pugin the younger.

Here Edmund Schulze, head of the German firm of organ-builders, lived with the Kennedys for several months in the autumn of 1869 while carrying out the delicate process of "finishing" each of the 3,603 pipes to suit its surroundings - for no musical instrument is more sensitive to the acoustics of the building than is a pipe organ.

After seven years, owing to the illness of Mrs Kennedy and the dampness of the organ house, the organ was sold to the Misses Carter, of Harrogate, who lent it to their newly-built Church of St Peter, where it remained for only two years because of dissatisfaction on the part of the vicar with the terms of the loan. So, once again, the instrument was offered for sale and fortunately it was untouched tonally.

The new Church of St Bartholomew at Armley had been consecrated in 1877, although without its tower and spire. The Schulze organ was purchased by Mr Henry William Eyres and presented to the church in 1879, enriched by two additional stops by the Schulze firm and a magnificent walnut case, standing on a vaulted stone screen in the north transept.

England has many fine organs built by skilled craftsmen, but in spite of technical advances unknown to Schulze, his masterpiece at Armley never fails to thrill the listener, whether by the grandeur and magnificence of the Great Swell and Pedal organs, or by the beauty and delicacy of the stops of the Choir and Echo organs.

As a visiting organist once said: "It is the cohesion that makes this organ."

A bridestone above Dovedale and Staindale by K. Paver.

Face on stone, Urra Moor on the Cleveland Hills.

Below, Pickering Castle from the shell-keep by Geoffrey Wright.

Chapter 5

Some Yorkshire Follies

Creating a prominent structure which had no practical value was not simply an ego-trip for one of the old-time landowners; quite often, it was to provide jobs for local men during periods when trade was slack.

Druid's Temple

High on the moors, between Ilton and Healey - and just a few miles from Malham - is one of the least known and visited of Yorkshire's curiosities: a Druid's Temple (built in the early part of last century!).

The temple stands on what is now Forestry Commission

land, in a part known as Druid's Plantation. The main part of the temple is oval in shape, about 100 feet long by 50 feet wide. The axis lies roughly in a north-south line. Some of the stones are massive, the tallest being about ten feet high. Scattered over the moor are several other stoneworks, although most are insignificant in comparison with the main structure.

The scheme is attributed to William Danby, descendant of a family who acquired the lordship of Masham during the reign of Henry VIII. Danby, born in 1752, occupied Swinton Hall, the family seat. A man deeply concerned in local affairs, Danby became High Sheriff of Yorkshire in 1784.

Much of Danby's time was spent in an extensive re-building of the mansion. Included in the work was a fine library and a museum which housed a comprehensive mineral collection. The poet Southey, in one of his tours, was entertained at Swinton by William Danby in 1829.

Danby had a great love of building for its own sake. Perhaps, at Ilton, he just wanted to build something that was different. A greater possibility is that his project provided work for the local inhabitants who might otherwise have been unemployed and gone hungry.

G. Firth (1963)

Wainhouse Tower

Wainhouse Tower, perched high on the hillside overlooking the Vale of Calder, on the outskirts of Halifax, has always been a bit of a mystery. No one really knows exactly how it came to dominate the skyline and it is the subject of many local tales.

There it stands, all 300 feet of it, offering an amazing panorama of town and moorland scenery from its quaintly ornamented high balcony. To reach this breathtaking vantage point, one must scale some 400 stone steps, which gradually wind the visitor up through the gloomy interior, which is illuminated only by an occasional window.

Once a year, members of the public are allowed to make the climb of a famous landmark and one of the strangest of architectural follies, which is believed to have originally been a tall chimney to disperse the smoke, carried up the hillside by an underground flue, from a dyeworks in the valley below.

Legend has it that, when the dyeworks ceased to operate, a Mr Wainhouse decided to convert the chimney into an ornamental tower and secured the services of an Italian architect who designed the present column around the chimney.

The most popular story about Wainhouse Folly is that it was erected as a result of a feud between the Wainhouse family and the Edwards family of Pye Nest Estate.

The Edwards' land was situated down in the valley and, having reason to suspect the Wainhouses of being "Peeping Toms", they erected a huge wall to blot out their neighbour's view. Not to be outdone, Mr Wainhouse had the huge tower built so that he would have an even better view into Pye Nest - much to the chagrin of the unfortunate Edwards.

Yet another strange story credits the amazing Mr Wainhouse with being one of the pioneers in smoke abatement. It tells how the tower was originally a chimney built to collect and disperse all the smoke from the homes and mills of the little manufacturing town of Sowerby Bridge, situated in the valley.

Just how the plan was to operate, we shall never know. Perhaps, after the chimney was built, the problem of collecting the smoke from the town proved too difficult to solve.

The latest mystery to be associated with Wainhouse

Tower concerned a bucket, which was discovered to be balanced on the top of the 15 ft lightning conductor. It appeared overnight. Halifax Parks Committee, who are responsible for the tower, said it could stay there for ever rather than risk someone's life. But one day it went.

It could at least be claimed that Halifax had Yorkshire's highest bucket.

J. Tempest (1961)

Yorke's Folly

At the heathery rim of Nidderdale, above Bewerley, are the remains of a structure which testifies to the good nature of a family who lived in the valley for 400 years, only to have their possessions sold as recently as the 1920s for the payment of estate duties: a fate that befell many other Yorkshire families in the period between the wars.

Yorke's Folly, on Guiscliffe, had its origins in another period of privation, the mid-18th century. This time it was the dalesfolk who were suffering in a period of bad weather and general unemployment. John Yorke, of Bewerley, a major landowner of the upper dale, commissioned the work to provide employment, and thus income, for impoverished craftsmen.

A gale in the 1890s toppled much of the folly. Enough

remains to commemorate a family which won its lands through purchase rather than conquest and which itself knew hard times, suffering from swingeing fines imposed by the Star Chamber for its Catholic sympathies.

The Yorkes sprang into prominence in Nidderdale following the Dissolution of the Monasteries. Their Dales estate ultimately extended to over 16,000 acres. They were content to live quietly, as rural squires, with an inclination towards the sporting life.

Just when Yorke's Folly was constructed is not known. The John Yorke who was concerned with it was married about the year 1740. Another feature of the moor which was for long a focal point of attention is the Crocodile Stone, resembling the reptile's head - a piece of gritstone, naturally sculptured, which stands just across the road from the Folly but is now almost obliterated by bracken.

The Nidderdale Yorkes had their Edwardian sunset when Bewerley Hall - and half of Nidderdale - were presided over by the Old Squire, Thomas Edward Yorke. This indomitable man married twice, having a large family by his first wife and being married to his second wife sufficiently long for them to celebrate their silver wedding anniversary. He walked to Ramsgill when he was aged 82 and on his death, 10 years later, he was referred to as the Last Squire.

W. R. Mitchell (1982)

Polly Peachum's Tower

On the lower slopes of Penhill, in the direction of Wensley and about a mile from Bolton Hall across the river, stands a picturesque ruin known as Polly Peachum's Tower, which takes its name from Lavinia Fenton, who took the party of Polly in Gay's *Beggar's Opera* on the London stage in 1728.

She became first the mistress and then the wife of the 3rd Duke of Bolton, who built the tower for her. It was used as a summer house and it is said that when she sang there, her voice could be heard at Bolton Hall.

She apparently behaved discreetly and was much loved by the Duke, although Lady Mary Wortley Montagu made the following tart comment about her - "bred in an alehouse and produced on the stage: found the way to be esteemed. So useful is early experience!"

W. W. Thurlow (1977)

Moorland Mansion

Castle Carr has a commanding position on the edge of bleak and barren moorland at the head of Luddenden Dean, near Halifax. Black, and somewhat forbidding, though in stately Norman and Elizabethan styles, it was completed in 1872.

History leaves many loopholes in the story of Castle Carr. It does not record why its builder chose such a remote spot to erect such a fine building - fine in those days, but completely out of place in modern times.

Castle Carr, standing on the site of a farmhouse of the same name, was the idea of Joseph Priestley Edwards. Construction work was stopped for some time when he lost his life in the Abergele railway disaster of 1868. It was later taken up by his son, who for a short period occupied the hall.

Forty thousand tons of local stone were used and items of special interest in the design include Norman arches, a portcullis, a banqueting hall 56ft by 28ft, picture gallery, stone carvings, statues, in-laid ceilings and many bedrooms and bathrooms. In the grounds are ornamental lakes and five fountains - the third highest in the country and among the most spectacular.

Only two years after completion, Castle Carr was put up for auction, but withdrawn at £36,000. Again in 1889, the Castle came under the auctioneer's hammer, but then the best offer was £24,000.

Recently, the seventh owner of the property in under 100 years sold it by auction in several lots. The long task of dismantling it has begun. The lakes will remain but soon the site of Castle Carr will be no more than a large gravel patch.

E. Riley (1962)

Chapter 6

Storied Stones

Almost every stone has a story to tell. Here is an account of a memorial to a group of patriotic waggoners, a bridge about which a romantic tale is told and details of a married couple's grave in which they were to be separated by water.

Waggoners Went to War

Sir Mark Sykes, sixth Baronet of Sledmere, in the East Riding, raised the Waggoners' Reserve Corps in 1912 from the local farm men and secured its recognition as a military unit. The story is told on the ornate war memorial which stands in the village.

This memorial was made with a circular centre on which were carved the sequence of events just before and during the 1914-18 war. The stone carving is surrounded by four ornamental columns, each being different from the others.

The events recorded are a plan of the course of the waggoners' annual driving competitions, leading the corn, joining the Waggoners' Reserve, receiving mobilisation papers, saying farewell to the family, on board troopship, disembarking, warfare, with the munition wagons - and Germans in retreat.

Here is an extract from stanzas composed by Sir Mark Sykes and inscribed on the memorial:

> *When from these Wolds twelve hundred men*
> *Came forth from field and fold and pen*
> *To stand against the law of might,*

To labour and to die for right
And for to save the world from wrong,
To shield the weak and bind the strong.

P.L.

Beggar's Bridge

Around the Beggar's Bridge, which crosses the river Esk in Glaisdale, is woven a legend which may not be true but is romantic.

In the 17th century, Tom Ferris, a youth of modest means, fell in love with Squire Richardson's daughter, Agnes, who lived on the other side of the Esk, but father frowned on the affair. His daughter, he declared, would never marry a beggar, but he added the rider that if Tom ever became a man of means, the matter would be re-considered.

So Tom decided to go to foreign parts to make his fortune and arranged a final visit to his sweetheart on the eve of his departure. Alas, the river was in high flood and as there was no bridge there, he could not cross the river. The fond farewells went unspoken.

Tom went off the next day, made his fortune, came home, married Agnes and built the bridge for the benefit of future generations. As proof of all this, Tom's initials, T.F., and the date 1621, adorn the bridge. Tom became mayor of Hull.

H. J. S. (1950)

A Watery Grave

In the churchyard at Kirkby Malham is a grave with a small watercourse down the middle. The grave is said to be of a sea captain and his wife, whose married life was not very happy because he was away from home a great deal.

When he died, his wife - in her understandable bitterness - said that as water had parted them in life, so it should in death. The grave was designed accordingly.

The old lady left it in her will that as her husband had been buried on one side of the water, she had to be buried on the other side. But when she died, and her grave was being dug, solid rock was found under the sod.

A conference took place, during which it was suggested that the rock should be blasted. This was rejected for fear of disturbing the other graves. So the wife was buried on the same side of the grave as her husband.

M. Waddington (1950)

Blacksmith's Epitaph

The churchyard at Old Malton contains a tombstone relating to William Hope, who died in 1761, aged 63 years. He must have been a blacksmith, for the stone bears the following curious inscription:

> *His Soul, I hope, in Heaven at Rest,*
> *In Singing Praises with the Blest.*
> *The 5 Psalm to be sung at his Funeral.*
> *My Sledge and hammer lie reclined,*
> *My Bellows, too, have lost their Wind,*
> *My Fire's extinct, my Forge decay'd,*
> *And in the Dust my Vice is laid,*
> *My Coal is Spent, My Iron's gone,*
> *My Nails are Drove, my Work is Done;*
> *My Fire Dry'd Corpse lies here at Rest,*
> *My Soul, Smoak-like, is*
> *Soaring to be Blest.*
>
> *Edgar Brown*

Chapter 7

Fabulous Dishes

It's your stomach 'at 'ods your back up! Yorkshire folk have their local partialities, quite apart from Yorkshire pudding, the first of which - "they" say - was made by an angel.

Freshwater Lobsters

Crayfish are to be found in most of our Dales rivers. Yore, Wharfe, Aire and Ribble are fairly well stocked in their deeper, stony stretches, though nowadays few people will be acquainted with the freshwater lobsters, except anglers, who find them a source of annoyance when bait fishing in the evenings.

It would also seem they are fairly numerous in such inland sheets of water as Malham Tarn and Semerwater. Once, we had a good haul of perch from the tarn and almost without exception they had crayfish in their stomaches. One fish, weighing 1½lb had eaten no fewer than eight. The same year we camped on the shores of Semerwater and one morning found more than 100 dead bream and rudd near the side. Each corpse was being attacked by crayfish and some had been half eaten from the tail upwards.

So far as I have been able to ascertain, it is only in the Yore that crayfish are protected. Both the Wensleydale and the Hawes and High Abbotside Angling Associations have a by-law that stipulates "the crayfishing season shall begin on August 10th and end on September 30th. Any person not being the holder of an Association ticket shall be charged 1s for a crayfishing ticket."

Only the claws and flappers contain edible flesh, and the former have to be cracked with a hammer. One of the natives said: "Tis a fiddling job for so hard an eat."

I went on a crayfishing expedition, setting off about teatime with a lump of liver which was to serve as bait. The liver was cut into six pieces, tied to a yard of string and stick, and then moved to the bank, each bait resting on the river bottom about a yard from the side. By the time the last one was in position, a crayfish was sampling the first.

At the outset, only ones and twos were collected, but gradually the liver enticed the crayfish from their hiding places. Slowly but surely they ambled around or over the stones to the feast. There were 14 at one bait and all but two were safely netted. Six dozen or more crayfish were collected before we ceased operations.

The record haul, made some 60 years ago, stands to the credit of Sproates Blades, who was commissioned to provide 1,000 live crayfish for the stocking of a Scottish reservoir. He and another man had £10 for the job. They obtained the required number in one evening under two hours. Overnight, the fish were kept alive in bags sunk in Gayle Beck. They made the journey next day by train in milk cans.

What is more, not a single crayfish died on the way.

T. K. Wilson (1943)

Ribston Pippin

The ancestor of the Ribston Pippin, a famous variety of apple tree, is to be seen in the grounds of Ribston Park near Wetherby.

Records indicate that in 1709, Sir Henry Goodriche

planted some pips from apples grown in Rouen, France, and three of them grew. Only one was deemed worth keeping. This became the original Ribston Pippin.

The trunk of the old tree was blown down in 1828. A sucker from the old roots was preserved and can still be seen.

(Or was, this note having been written over half a century ago).

Sydney Moorhouse (1941)

Champion Goosegogs

Don't enter the Egton Bridge Gooseberry Show unless your berry is the size of a plum. Ideally, it should be approaching the size of an egg.

The Egton Bridge Old Gooseberry Society operates, with a minimum of fuss, in a snug part of the Esk Valley, and has been in the "goosegog" business since 1800, with records dating back to the 1840s. The show is on the first Tuesday in August. Then you can see the heavyweights of the gooseberry tribe, all pampered and preened, set out on white plates to attract the admiring glances of members and visitors.

The fine points of showing "goosegogs" are not appreciated by strangers, one of whom looked startled when she overheard a committee man say to a companion: "There's a lot o' new maidens at t'far end this year." Maidenhood at the Eskdale show is a sort of probationary period. Only when you have won a trophy in a class for maidens can you compete in the major section.

Gooseberry talk ranged from the effects of recent weather on the crop to fanciful tales, such as the claim by a member of the society that one night a salmon crept out of the river and ate his best berries.

The "baddies" of the gooseberry world are the wasps. The insects with striped jumpers take a delight in waiting for the best berries to ripen before puncturing them. The prizes at Egton Bridge go to those who show "dry" berries. Many a potential champion has been jabbed by a wasp.

I several times asked if the popularity of gooseberry-growing had anything to do with the local soil. The sides of the dales are steep and close together. I half expected them to be terraced, as are the vineyards of the continent. But, no - soil doesn't really matter. It's a question of muck - good muck. "You give 'em plenty o' manure, if you have it. I never use nowt but farm manure."

At the show, weight is everything. A man might grow gooseberries fit for a Queen and as tangy as the best wine, but it avails him nothing if his berry is less than plum size. In a room adjacent to the hall - a room in which people whisper and tend to move on tip toe - the weighman uses scales which have to stand in room temperature for three hours before being used. The balance is given its final cheque using feathers.

In 1952, the champion - Tom Ventress - caused a minor sensation with a berry which weighed 30 drams 8 grains (at one time they assessed a berry's worthiness in "pennyweights").

As soon as one show is over, the members think about the next. Their selected trees (as they are called at Egton Bridge) are pruned so hard about November that no one could conceal a baby under one of them.

W. R. Mitchell (1980)

Denby Dale Pie

It's a good job that Yorkshire is the County of Broad Acres or it would never be able to contain the latest Giant Denby Dale Pie. Saturday, September 3rd, is the day to remember, when an estimated 40,000 portions of pie will be consumed.

The dish will be large enough to contain the huge once used for the last pie in 1964. Then, the pie dish was 18ft long, 6ft wide, 18in deep - and was launched as a ship, the SS Denby Dale, on a local canal. It was skippered by pretty girls and aboard was a smattering of VIPs, and the Press and TV cameramen were out in force.

The 1988 the pie celebrated 200 years of pie-making. Up to 100,000 people swamped Denby Dale over the two-day event. Only one pie ever went wrong and that was buried in quick lime in Toby Wood.

That was in 1887, when a recipe of beef, veal, lamb, pork, rabbits, hares, pigeons, grouse, ducks, plover, turkey, geese, suet and potatoes commemorated Queen Victoria's golden jubilee. Too much game had been used and hot and cold ingredients were mixed together. Also, they had engaged professional bakers - a fatal flaw!

When the pie was opened, the birds did not begin to sing - and the terrible stench sent onlookers falling over each other in a desperate attempt to escape the foul aroma.

Nevertheless, Denby Dalers, always ready to see the funny side of life, had black-edged "In Memoriam" funeral cards for the ill-fated pie printed, to raise funds that should have been made from selling the pie.

How did the tradition of Giant Pies begin? Well, ever patriotic, it was first suggested in 1788, as a thanksgiving for the recovery from mental illness of George III. Not until 1815 was another baked, to celebrate the defeat of Napoleon at Waterloo. Small by later standards, that pie was a mixture of mutton and fowl - two sheep and twenty fowls, with half a peck of flour used for the crust.

Hazel Wheeler (1988)

Dock Pudding

Claims were staked out and numbered notices warned outsiders to "keep off" and guard dogs were around to frighten off any determined "claim jumpers".

The casual visitor to the Calder Valley could have been forgiven for supposing that the locals had struck gold; in fact, the claims were to a much rarer treasure - *Polygonum bistota*, or the sweet dock, an essential ingredient in a local breakfast delicacy called Dock Pudding.

It was the day of the world's first dock pudding championship. Forty-two ladies and four gentlemen assembled at Hebden Bridge's Charlton Ballroom to compete for the honour of being the world's champion dock pudding maker. Each came along bearing a pot containing a brew made from two pounds of the rare sweet docks which had been well corralled during the weeks before.

The winner, Mrs Betty Horsfall, stung other competitors and pleased the judges by leaving out the nettles from her pudding. Those judges looked dubious as they sampled the pudding.

The championship was only part of a Calder Valley Arts Festival and will be held every two years. The year in between will give time for the ravaged dock pastures to renew their lustre. As one local put it: "They will need all that; the hillsides were stripped bare."

Chris Laws (1971)

A horn is blown to announce the completion of the Penny Hedge in Whitby Harbour. Photographer not known.

The Swastika carving on Ilkley Moor by Edwin Mitchell.

Right, Lanercost Priory by Leonard Jackson.

Chapter 8

Things that go Bump...

Your average Yorkshireman/woman has a realistic attitude to life, with little time for fantasy. Yet some people in Airedale did believe there were fairies at Cottingley, and shivers passed down the spines of some Dalesfolk at the mention of boggarts in potholes and an allusion to the bar-guest - a hound with eyes as big as saucers - in Trollers Gill.

Wee Folk at Cottingley

Sir Arthur Conan Doyle, the distinguished writer and creator of Sherlock Holmes, firmly believed in the existence of fairies in Yorkshire. The story of how this came about is recounted in *Fairies*, by Edward L. Gardner (Theosophical Publishing House, London).

In May, 1920, Mr Gardener received through the post two quarter-plate negatives on glass purporting to be photographs of fairies. One showed several figures dancing in front of a little girl and the other was of a gnome-like creature near a girl's beckoning hand.

He assumed they were forgeries but had them examined by an expert on faked photography and by Kodak's. Both these authorities pronounced that the photographs showed no signs of being faked works.

Mr Gardener went to see a Mrs Wright, of Cottingley, near Bradford, who had sent him the plates. He found that in 1917, Frances Griffiths, then ten years old, a young cousin of the Wrights, had come from South Africa to stay with them for the summer. Both pictures had been taken in the glen near the house. Elsie, then 13 years old, the daughter of Mr and Mrs Wright, took the first one and in it was Frances. In the second photograph the positions had been reversed.

The girls had used Mr Wright's camera and he had developed the plates, but not at any time had he believed their story that they had frequently met, and eventually photographed, fairies in the glen. He thought the girls had made the figures out of paper.

In the summer of 1920, Frances again came to stay at Cottingley and the girls took three more photographs of the fairies. This time, two cameras were given to them from an outside source and the plates were secretly marked, but again exhaustive tests failed to reveal any indications of forgery.

Conan Doyle kept in constant touch with these developments. The Christmas, 1920, issue of the *Strand Magazine* contained an article by him and Mr Gardner entitled "An Epoch-making Event - Fairies Photographed". The issue sold out within three days and the story spread round the world.

During the summer of 1921, the girls, who were both clairvoyants, again spent several hours in the glen, this time accompanied by Geoffrey Hodson, an expert clairvoyant. They saw a large number of fairies, and other similar creatures, some of them being life-size. Others were playing games to the accompaniment of music or seemingly praying but they were all too translucent to be photographed.

The Cottingley photographs are unique, although many well-known and reputable people claim to have seen spirits. It seems that the perfect mediumistic qualities of Frances coupled with the fact that both girls were good simple clairvoyants, quite unspoilt because unaware of it, produced a rare combination which, completely by chance, succeeded.

> *From a book review (1965)*
> *The photographs of Cottingley fairies were*
> *subsequently revealed to be fakes.*

A Dales Boggart

The courting couple who walked near Hurtle Pot in Chapel-le-Dale, one evening, were local people who no doubt knew about the boggart, which was supposed to live at the bottom of the broad 58ft gash in the limestone. They may have heard that this boggart had a habit of drowning people in the 20ft deep pool.

They were quite unprepared for the unearthly noises which suddenly arose from the tree-shaded pothole. The two visitors fled in terror. Not long afterwards, a man clambered from Hurtle Pot and made his way back to Weathercote House, where he was staying with the Metcalfe family. He was carrying a flute and, like Orpheus, had been playing in the underworld!

The tale was jotted down by a traveller named Walter White, who heard that "in olden times the boggart's deeds were terrible, but of late years he only frightens people with noises.

"Both this and Jingle Pot are choked with water from subterranean channels in flood time, and then there is heard here such an intermittent throbbing, gurgling noise, accompanied by what seems dismal gaspings, that a timorous listener might easily believe the boggart was drowning his victims."

B. T. (1966)

A Phantom Mill

Folk lore is usually lost or forgotten. Seldom is it destroyed. Yet potholers who went to Robin Hood's Mill, near Stainforth, in North Ribblesdale, in the 1930s, were blamed for stopping some old grindstones from turning deep in the earth.

The shaft, which lay near the river, on the west bank, just above the packhorse bridge, had been known as the "Mill" for generations. A local legend stated that a mill stood here. The miller, not content with making a great deal of money during the week, once kept his grindstones turning on the Sabbath Day.

As a punishment for his breach of the Commandment, the mill sank out of sight, and a low murmuring sound which came from the sink-hole was said to be the noise of the mill-stones still grinding away. Before the potholers began their exploration, they were warned by a clergyman that in trying to solve the mystery they might destroy the romance associated with it.

The potholers excavated the hole to a depth of over ten feet, and the rumbling sound was then to be heard. Later, the rumbling ceased. The phantom mill ground away no more.

W. R. Mitchell (1966)

The Barguest

If there was a characteristically Yorkshire visitant, it was the barguest - a large beast with eyes as big as saucers.

This was very much a spirit in animal form. It could be a dog of supernatural size and terrifying appearance or else it could come in the form of a bear, a mastiff dog or any other animal.

It was only very occasionally that barguests were disposed to be playful. Usually they came as harbingers of approaching death. Only those soon about to die could see them, but if you touched a companion he would instantly experience the same vision as yourself. To go out to look for a barguest, instead of seeing it accidentally, was to court instant death.

As lately as 1881, a man at Appletreewick in Wharfedale went out to confront the barguest of Trollers Gill. Next morning, his body was found by shepherds, with such marks inflicted on it as could have been made by no mortal creature.

Carson I. A. Ritchie (1984)

Chapter 9

At Random

The pages of *"The Dalesman"* contain many examples of the keen observation of our readers.

Peephole at Burnsall

The school at Burnsall, in Wharfedale, was founded by William Craven in 1603. The interior contained - until 1965 at least - much fine woodwork. Upstairs there was a wooden wall between the master's room and the boys' dormitories. There was no internal access between the rooms.

High up on the wall was a small slit, hardly visible without close inspection. This must have enabled the master to view his pupils without them being aware of the fact. The smoothness of the aperture points to the frequent use of the device.

Ivy Booker

"Luck" at Catwick

The most curious thing which I have seen in Yorkshire was hanging on the door of the blacksmith's shop at Catwick, near Hull. It was a board about a foot square on which were nailed a number of farthings.

Each farthing represented a member of the village who went to serve in the 1914-18 war. As each husband, son or father departed, his family took along a farthing to John Hugill to be nailed on the board.

Whether or not "luck" could be claimed to be attached to the farthing-board, it is hard to say, but each farthing-man came back from the war and only one was wounded, in the arm. I can still remember as a child begging my father to tell me which was his farthing.

The smithy is closed now and old John Hugill sleeps in the churchyard. I still remember my curio.

Barbara Robinson

A Hamlet called Booze

Booze stands on a hill end some 600 feet about Arkle Beck. A few farms and cottages catch the eye of the sun and are truly exposed to winter gales. There is but one road: steep, constricted and winding. As the road reaches the edge of the hamlet of Booze, the tarmac peters out, to be succeeded by a rough track, the centre of which is tufty with grass.

A J Brown wrote: "Booze, despite its encouraging name, is about the most teetotal hamlet I have ever explored hopefully, from end to bitter end." If you visit Booze and I recommend you to walk there, not drive, on the final mile of road and track. Do not expect to see signs of drunkenness. Booze lacks an inn and its 19th century history was closely bound up with Methodists, who favoured abstinence.

The name is the most unlovely aspect of the place. Booze is a corruption of "Bowehous", an Old English name meaning "the house by the bow or curve". The local postman invited me to say "bowhouse" quickly a few times, and then add the Dales intonation. I found myself uttering the word "booze".

During a long and unexciting history the place has dedicated itself to farming and lead mining. The lead mine in nearby Faggerhill, a Norse name, had over 25 miles of rails. Down by Arkle Beck, which drains Arkengarthdale, is the entrance to Booze Wood Level, which was driven northwards to encounter the profitable Booze Vein.

A local farmer recalled the families who were at Booze 50 years ago. They bore well known Dales surnames like Hird, Hutchinson, Coates, Harper and Longstaff. Those were the days when the summer pastures were grazed by Shorthorn cattle, the milk from which was converted, through the efforts of farmers' wives and daughters, into butter and cheese. They were delivered to the shop in Langthwaite for conveyance to Richmond.

In spring, waste ground is bright with clumps of yellow mountain pansies. Elsewhere, spring sandwort, which is tolerant to lead, shows its tiny, star shaped white flowers. The summer meadows are bright with buttercups.

The postman mentioned the old days, when each little Dales community lived very much to itself and was clannish. The old time barriers between native and off comer have largely broken down. But there are still folk who have never heard of Booze...

W R Mitchell (1979)

Kirkdale Cave

Beyond Helmsley, where the road sweeps a great wide curve towards Pickering and the Yorkshire coast, a signpost with a solitary finger points the way to St Gregory's Minster and to historic Kirkdale. There are older things in Kirkdale than the famous church and other Saxon remains.

Across Hodge Beck, where it is forded by the road, is a tiny quarry and the twin apertures of a cave. It is now quite empty. It was once piled high with bones.

At the beginning of the 19th century, this fact was brought to the notice of the University of Oxford authorities whose interest in the area began in 1659 when the Minster church was bequeathed to them by the will of Henry Danvers, Earl of Danby. An examination of the cave and its contents was undertaken by Dr William Buckland, professor of mineralogy, and his findings caused quite a stir in natural history circles. The bones were found to be those of lions, tigers, bears and bison, as well as several smaller animals such as wolves and hyenas.

The many hundred hyena bones led Buckland to suppose that the cave was formerly a hyena den and that the larger animals had been brought in piecemeal to provide food for the occupants.

At what period of history did lions and tigers roam the forests of England? Bede, in his Ecclesiastical History of the English Nation, says of the site chosen by Cedd for his monastery here that it was a craggy place looking more like the lurking place of robbers and the lairs of wild beasts than a habitation of man. The cave beasts were infinitely older.

J A Clough (1963)

Park Rash

I consulted books about the Dales. Hardly any of them mentioned Park Rash at length and the other references were simply testifying to its existence and its grim reputation as a motor route between upper Wharfedale and Coverdale.

The name itself is not without interest. "Park" suggests an area which, in medieval times, was set aside for deer. In 1409, the Earl of Westmorland was granted a warren park, plus a lodge. The Earl had the misfortune to associate himself with the rebels in the Pilgrimage of Grace; his estates were confiscated, and the area around what we now call Park Rash was divided into two... the parks of West Scale and East Scale. The word "scale" comes from the Norse and means a steep hill. "Rash" also means a hill. You have been warned!

The derelict dwelling on great Hunters Sleet at 1,654 ft, is referred to on old maps as the Grouse House but may, when first built, have accommodated coal miners. Veins of brittle coal were located in the Yoredale Series of rocks. Park Rash was a celebrated proving ground for early cars and motor bikes. When a Whit Monday endurance race took place between London and Newcastle, the route lay over Park Rash.

Kit Wiseman and a friend stationed themselves near the steep section, with two horses and chains, prepared to help out any luckless competitor. Alec Jackson, of Keighley, was a star when motor cycles were being ridden up the hill. Alec usually stood on the saddle of his motor cycle as he began his rapid climb. As Jim, son of Kit Wiseman, told me: "Folk used to fair gape at him."

W R Mitchell (1981)

Buried at Ainderby

A few weeks ago, one of my parishioners, digging for a waterpipe, found some bones. This may not seem so remarkable but when he came across a considerable number with an almost intact skull, he began to take notice. He knew, and it is not without significance, that within a few hundred yards of where he was digging was a 13th century Chapel of Ease. Land was granted in 1253 and prayers were to be said on specified days for the souls of Picot de Lascelles, Adam and Avis, their ancestors and their heirs.

Consequently, our amateur archaeologist no doubt thought he had found the monks' burial ground and, to be on the safe side, he informed the police. This was on a Sunday, and from then on there was much activity. The local constable was on leave so his neighbouring colleague had to cycle many miles to make a preliminary examination.

When he was convinced that the bones were human and in large numbers, telephone wires and police radios hummed with activity. The remains were removed by the police, and the whole affair was placed in official hands. The same day I was informed by the assisting constable about what had happened. I was asked to arrange for the bones to be decently re-buried in the churchyard.

What happened in the next few weeks I do not know. I assume that the lists of missing persons from the parish of Ainderby Steeple and surrounding areas would be carefully scrutinised. In the churchyard, weeks later, were the local constable, the undertaker who had made the coffin, the sexton and vicar.

An impressive official document, giving authority from the proper quarter, for the decent re-interment of an unknown person was opened. An "unknown person" can conjure much in the imagination. Was he a monk or rich man or poor man? We do not know. His remains are in our churchyard.

F L (1968)

Nomads of the Wolds

The Wold Rangers were an unusual type of vagrant who roamed the Yorkshire Wolds from around the middle of the 19th century until the 1930s. Odd ones may have lingered after that date. They, unlike gipsies, were loners, preferring their own company, living rough in woods or hedgerows in summer and seeking shelter in barns or haylofts in the winter.

Many came to the Wolds from other parts of England.

Odd ones came from abroad, probably because there was always work to be found on the large Wold farms. Most of the Wold Rangers liked a drink, and after being paid by the farmer would often be absent from work, especially on Monday mornings.

At harvest time, three or four of these men might be seen working on the same farm. As well as the pay (around half a crown a day) they received their "looances", a word used to this day "allowance", the ration of three gills of beer for each farm worker.

My husband remembers some of the Wold Rangers who were frequent visitors to his father's and grandfather's farms in the 1920s. They had nicknames, some obviously referring to characteristics or deformities. Cloggy Sam could entertain by tap dancing. There was no doubt where Mad Halifax came from! Horse Hair Jack must have had a sideline in selling hair but is also remembered for throwing an axe in a temper while chopping sticks. Three fingered Jimmy was short tempered, and Cuddy had a squeaky voice. Cut Lip Sam was a somewhat unkind name, as he was disfigured by a hare lip. Others were Stamp, Tom Frod, Long Charlie and Spanish Prince, the latter being dark and swarthy.

The one my husband remembers best - in fact, I myself met him in the 1930s - was Tommy Rook. I heard that he ended his days at a home in the Driffield area. Tommy called himself a "Gentleman Tramp" and took pride in his appearance. He waxed his moustache and always had a change of clothing, washing his shirts and drying them on a hedge. His boots were well polished and he looked very different from the other usually dirty and bedraggled Wold Rangers. Tommy liked his liquor. Any money he saved soon disappeared after a spell on the bottle.

Around Christmas, it was not unknown for the Rangers to commit some small crime, such as stealing a bike, in order to be given a short prison sentence. They would thus be fed and had a roof over their heads until the days became lighter and warmer in the spring.

Irene Megginson (1977)

Saltersgate Inn

One had but to mention the world "smugglers" to be assured of an attentive audience. Those picturesque law-breakers, with their cutlasses and pistols, their nocturnal comings and goings and their ceaseless efforts to evade the preventive men, will always appeal to the romantically minded.

To link such illicit dealings with any particular hostelry is to invest it with a historic interest which places it in a class by itself. The North East Moors of Yorkshire can boast of at least one such place. Saltersgate lies on the wild but beautiful road about mid-way between Pickering and Whitby. Sheltered from the east by the frowning mass of Whinny Nab, it is separated from the Hole of Horcum on the south by Gallows Dike (what a place for a gallows; the stone base is still there).

It is really called the "Wagon and Horses", but to the thousands of travellers who call and sample its true Yorkshire hospitality it will always be Saltersgate Inn. Smuggling did take place here, which is the reason why the locality became known as Saltersgate.

The article smuggled was salt - just ordinary common salt, needed for preserving the farmer's pork and, at the coast, the catches of fish not needed for immediate consumption. Kegs of brandy and hollands which had eluded the eye of the preventive men, also found their way here.

Salt was scarce and heavily taxed. Fishermen on the North East coast could not afford to buy it and therefore depended largely on the smuggled variety. It is believe they transported fish to the inn on horseback and salted the fish free from the eyes of the revenue officers.

Saltersgate was well-known as a coaching inn. A farrier shod the horses of the stage coaches. I talked with a former landlord who said that in his youth he had known, and often talked with, the old farrier, who readily admitted that he had made a pretty penny out of shoeing the ponies of adventurous fishermen.

Gilbert Creighton (1955)

Walls of Jericho

It was milk and biscuit time. I decided to profit from the silence and read a Bible story to my new class of six-year-olds. I chose the one about Joshua and the Walls of Jericho and was surprised by the sudden upsurge of interest.

"I've been to Jericho," called several voices. "And Jerusalem." They might have added: "Egypt, Moscow and World's End" for they are all within a three mile radius at the west end of Thornton. A friend on the staff kindly offered to drive me round the village where I had taken up my first teaching post.

The village of Thornton, which was incorporated with the City of Bradford in 1899, lies on hilly ground. There are two valleys, each with its stream. Pinchbeck Valley is crossed by a huge railway viaduct and Pitty Beck flows along the other valley. These two streams unite to form Bradford Beck.

Along Wells Head Road is Jerusalem Farm. It is said that soldiers long ago named Moscow, Egypt and Jericho after outposts where they were stationed. "Moscow" and "Jerusalem" are small hamlets, the latter with its own chapel, the stones of which are now built into a private house. The area is windy and stony, with a sweeping view of small, black-walled fields. Haworth, only six miles away, seems closer in spirit.

The Walls of Jericho, built as retaining walls to quarry works, are quite impressive. They enclose a narrow road and rise steeply on either side - huge black blocks of millstone grit. It was as short but eerie experience to walk between them.

J Stone (1979)

Dearbought Field

"Where shall we go for our walk?" "Over the fields to Austwick."

This decision always gave me a thrill during my childhood holidays at Clapham, particularly when Uncle Bob was one of the party, enlivening the way with his anecdotes and local lore, in which Austwick was particularly rich.

What child could fail to be entranced, for instance, by the famous half-way stone which gets up and turns round every Christmas Eve when it hears the Church clock strike twelve?

But there was one tale which made a deep impression on my mind, perhaps because Uncle Bob's reminiscences were so rarely sombre. Just past the half-way stone came the sharp command: "Halt! Eyes right!" in tones reminiscent of his old Volunteer days.

"Yonder," he would declaim, pointing with outstretched stick - "yonder lies Dearbought Field. Dost know how it came by its name?" After a short pause came the story.

"The man who owned yon field vowed to give it to another man if he could plough it in a day. No one thought it could be done; but the man did it by sundown, and at the end of the last furrow he dropped dead beside his plough.

'Twas his, he'd won it fairly, but in consideration of the price he'd paid the name was called Dearbought and Dearbought Field it is to this day."

We invariably walked on in silence for a while; but if the tale of the hard-won field cast a temporary shadow, it contained a moral which no listener was the worse for taking to heart.

Enid F Camm (1943)

Shoddy Kingdom

When Batley was my home town in the 1920s and 1930s, it was famous for two things - its rugby league football team which, way back in antiquity, had won the cup, and of course for shoddy, which was discovered in the town in 1813.

For the enlightenment of non-Yorkshiremen who have never heard of shoddy in any other connotation than what the Oxford dictionary unflatteringly defines as "counterfeit, pretentious, trashy: anything of worse quality than it claims or seems to have" - shoddy is a valuable textile raw material which brought about a sartorial revolution in the 19th century.

The use of it dramatically reduced the price of woollen clothing and brought it within the means of the working man and women for the first time in history. The attire of the workman became indistinguishable from that of his master - a social change of great significance.

Batley in 1813 was a completely rural area dotted with the cottages of the handloom weavers. The discoverer of shoddy was a man called Benjamin Law. He found that if old clothes made of wool were ground into a fibrous mass (shoddy) they could be mixed with virgin wool and re-manufactured into new cloth.

From 1813 onwards, assisted by the development of the power loom, shoddy mills sprang up all over the town and by 1850 there were over 30, most of them substantial three or four-storey buildings, each accommodating several hundred workpeople.

It took a couple of wars - the Crimean and the Franco-Prussian - to bring Batley's industrial expansion to its peak. Batley in the 1870s was a microcosm of Victorian England - a town of great industry and enterprise but also of great extremes of wealth and poverty. The manufacturers owned carriages and pairs and lived in great luxury in the select residential area known as Upper Batley. The workers lived in grim back-to-back terrace houses in the town, with twenty or more people sharing one outside privy.

This first generation of manufacturers was largely uneducated and some had to sign their cheques with a cross because they could neither read nor write. They competed with each other in their display of wealth, just as they competed in business, and every house which was built in Upper Batley was a little bigger and more grandiose than the last.

The story is told of one illiterate nouveau riche whose sole instruction to the local architect was to build him "t'biggest house in t'district." The architect asked him what aspect he would like. The manufacturer looked at him perplexed and asked if the last manufacturer's mansion to be built had an aspect. The architect said that all houses must have an aspect.

"Aye, well then," came the reply, "tha mun gi' me three."

Derrick Boothroyd (1978)

Church in a Field

England has many "lost" villages with only a church to remind us of their previous existence. This is the case at Lead, which stands alone in a field off the B.1217 road from Hook Moor to Towton and Tadcaster. It was rendered as Lied in the Domesday Book, which recorded that "Gunner had two carucates to be taxed and there may be three ploughs there..."

Lead Church was a private chapel, rather than a parish church. The old manor house and attendant buildings have gone but the isolated chapel of the most influential local family endures, thanks to those who have spent time and money on restoration.

Lead Church has its group of Friends and an annual service takes place here each May. It is sometimes known as the Ramblers' Church because ramblers and cyclists met here in the past and they helped to restore it in 1934.

On my latest visit, I parked where the road verge near "The Crooked Billet" inn had been flattened to concrete hardness by the cars of previous visitors. My pilgrimage to Lead Church was not arduous. It involved crossing the road and a bridge over Cock Beck, clambering over a wooden stile and taking a diagonal course across a field to where the building stood in grand isolation.

I bowed my head for most of the way, not because I was feeling penitent but because the field was littered with fresh sheep droppings. There was time to pause and look at the beck. After the Battle of Towton, the watercourse was said to run red with blood.

Lead Church, restored periodically over the years, has stout walls, a sound roof and a bell in a small tower to call the faithful to worship. The stone windows are a matching set. Some itinerant stonemasons would work here to a grand design.

The church has been in the care of the Redundant Churches Fund since 1980. It remains a consecrated building, so measures have been taken to fence against farm stock. A substantial fence at the east end marks where a chancel stood - a chancel which may have been as large as the church that remains. Perhaps there was once a small burial ground.

A wooden barrier protects the doorway from rubbing by sheep. (They use the barrier instead!) Years ago, if anyone left the door open, cows would enter. The mess had to be cleaned up using water carried across the field from Cock Beck.

To walk through the door is to have the profound experience of intruding on the 18th century, with evidence of much earlier times. Such is the feeling of peace in this solitary building, with walls thick enough even to muffle the bleating of sheep, that after ten minutes I felt I could have happily stayed there forever.

W R Mitchell (1989)

The Sweet Lass

Who was the "Sweet Lass of Richmond Hill", who features in the famous song? She was Frances I'Anson, who was born at Leyburn on October 17, 1766. Frances was the daughter of William I'Anson, a wealthy attorney, of Bedford Row, London, and Hill House, Richmond, Yorkshire.

Frances was wooed by Leonard McNalley (1752-1820),

an eloquent Irish barrister and a writer of some merit who was active in the political affairs of his country. It may well have been in an attempt to induce her to marry him against the wishes of her parents that the young patriot penned the words which have become world-famous.

Whatever the truth of the matter, McNalley's ardour carried the day, and the couple became man and wife at St George's, Hanover Square, on January 16, 1787.

The words of the poem were set to music by James Hook (1746-1827), who was organist at Vauxhall Gardens. This tribute to "a rose without a thorn" was first sung there in 1789 by Charles Benjamin Incleson (1763-1826), the leading tenor vocalist of his generation.

Unhappily, Frances McNalley died in Dublin when she was only 29, leaving a young son. Her husband later married Louisa, daughter of the Rev Robert Edgeworth.

In Yorkshire, a walnut tree in the grounds of Hill House, beneath which the lovers are said to have plighted their troth, was eventually cut down, but the wood was stored and in 1944 was built into a fireplace in the Town Clerk's Lodgings in French Gate.

In his book, "The Story of Richmond, Yorkshire" (1946), David Brooks writes that the town's noted Georgian Theatre Royal was opened in 1788, with all the locally important families present. The "Sweet Lass of Richmond Hill" was there among them - a bride of 21 - and, says the author, "I like to think that she was one of the elite that autumn evening and was escorted to her seat by the man whose love song will live as long as the town of its birth."

A H Robinson (1975)

Tales of (a Yorkshire) Hoffman

The Craven Lime Company had no difficulty in recruiting workers for its Hoffman kiln, which had been constructed in 1873 beside Winskill Rock, near the village of Langcliffe.

A working man was paid next to nothing for his efforts, but the alternative to work was the insufficiency of parish help and, in later times, the dole. Men could be found who did not complain about the heat and dust.

Mr Hoffman's type of kiln, devised in Germany, produced lime of the best quality. Two fires ceaselessly pursued each other within an oval shape, each fire taking six weeks to complete a circuit. It was a greedy kiln, demanding vast quantities of limestone (which was in block form, stacked by hand) and substantial amounts of coal (fed into the system from above).

The kiln also demanded blood, toil and sweat from the small band of devoted workers - men who put strips of leather across their hands before they dare handle the burnt lime and who toiled until the back of the head was a ginger hue and their clothes were drenched by sweat.

Smoke which billowed from a 75-yard high brick chimney testified to the manager and the shareholders that all was well. The main drawback from their point of view was the fact of it being labour-intensive, with a high wages bill.

The kiln itself is still intact and impresses those who see it by its size - 150 ft long and 48 ft wide. In its heyday it had sixteen chambers, each capable of holding 100 tons of stone. The chimney, 75 yards high and 22 feet wide at the base, tapered to 11ft, was of red brick construction, though the date 1873 was picked out in white bricks.

The big kiln at Craven Quarry was operating from 1873 until 1931 and from 1937 until the outbreak of war. Gone is the chimney. Perversely, it toppled of its own accord, unseen by human eyes, one foggy morning in 1952. It had already been prepared for demolition, which was delayed for 24 hours. The chimney, though unattended at the time it fell, took the desired course.

Grass now grows on the flat top of the kiln, where once bogeys delivered coal and where a small stack of new bricks stood ready to be used if part of the kiln collapsed. The railway dock beside the kiln, where trucks were filled with newly-burnt cobs of lime, is now partly filled with water which has drained from the silent quarry.

The Hoffman kiln is a notable piece of Victorian technology. Anyone who enters it today, with permission, finds that sort of calm, gloomy dignity to be experienced in a monastic church. There is beauty in the upsweeping lines of the brick arching.

W R Mitchell (1980)

Peasholm Park

The story of Peasholm Park at Scarborough begins in December, 1911, when the Corporation bought from the

Duchy of Lancaster the defunct Northstead Manor Estate, covering much of the resort's North Bay. As a plaque at the main entrance to Peasholm Park reminds us, one of the ways in which an M.P. can resign is to apply for the bogus stewardship of the Manor of Northstead - a route most recently taken by John Stonehouse in 1975.

The site of today's park was rough ground known as Tucker's Field, partly occupied by piggeries and allotments. Using unemployed men, Scarborough Corporation created the heart of today's park in only six months. With its lake, boathouse, cafe, flower beds and extensive rockery, it opened to the public on June 19, 1912.

Then, as now, a willow-pattern bridge linked the shore with Peasholm's island, which was formed by banking up the soil excavated to produce the bed of the encircling lake. During the work, the foundations of the original Northstead Manor were found.

What gives Peasholm Park its special character are its buildings, all in the Japanese style. How many of Peasholm's happy patrons realise that the park is a perfect Japanese fantasy, a place of architectural pilgrimage as well as family fun? It provides Britain's best example of the fashion for Japanese building which flourished fleetingly but charmingly early this century.

At first expressed most clearly in that distinctive bridge, the Japanese theme was keenly pursued by Scarborough after the 1914-18 war. The Corporation also embarked on an informal extension to the park, up Peasholm Glen, which then was known as Wilson's Wood.

The whole scheme was completed in 1929 by the erection of the pagoda on the summit of Peasholm island, which was specially heightened for the project. This bold move gave Scarborough a landmark, the novelty of which is still not fully appreciated.

In 1975, the Scarborough historian, Raymond Fieldhouse, drew attention to the unique combination of a pagoda crowning "a man-made mound, in a public park, in an English town in the 20th century."

The architect of the pagoda, 77-year-old George Alderson, still practises in Scarborough. He recalls that miniature pantiles for the pagoda were specially made at Boroughbridge and that the structure had to be anchored to a massive concrete plinth to secure it against North East gales.

Mr Alderson also designed Peasholm's entrance gates. They are Japanese, of course.

Harry Mead (1980)

Index

Ainderby Burials 69
Barguest 63
Beggar's Bridge 49
Beverley's White Rabbit 38
Blacksmith's Epitaph 50
Booze 65
Bridestones 13
Broad Acres 7
Burning of Bartle 30
Burnsall Peephole 64
Catwick Luck 65
Church in a Field 77
Civic Arms 15
Corpse Way 11
Cottingley Fairies 59
Cow and Calf Rocks 14
Cups and Rings 9
Dales Boggart 61
Dane's Dyke 10
Dearbought Field 74
Denby Dale Pie 56
Devil's Arrows 7
Devil's Knell 37
Dock Pudding 57
Druids Temple 41
Ebbing and Flowing Well 17
Egton Gooseberries 54
Freshwater Lobsters 52
Frith Stools 37
Gagates and Snakestones 18
Green Man Mystery 32
Gypsey Race 20
Hoffman (Tales of a) 80

Horngarth	25
Kiplingcotes Derby Day	27
Kirkdale Cave	67
Knareborough's Petrifying Well	16
Leeds Organ	39
Moorland Crosses	12
Moorland Mansion	46
Nine Tailors Make Man	29
Park Rash	68
Peasholm Park	81
Phantom Mill	62
Pickering Frescoes	35
Polly Peachum's Tower	45
Pulpits and Pews	36
Ribston Pippin	53
Ripon's Seven Hornblasts	23
Rudston's Magical Monolith	8
Saltersgate Inn	72
Scarborough's Hidden Wells	21
Scorton Arrow	26
Shoddy Kingdom	75
Sweet Lass of Richmond Hill	78
Swinnergill Kirk	34
Turkey Lecturn	39
Veronica Handkerchief	36
Waggoners at War	48
Wainhouse Tower	42
Walls of Jericho	73
Watery Grave	50
Wolds Rangers	70
Yorke's Folly	44

List of Illustrations

Page

- 4 Brimham Rocks by Bill Pates.
- 6 Young Ralph Cross near Blakey Ridge by Bernard Fearnley.
- 8 Rudston Monolith and Church by John Thomlinson.
- 12 White Cross near Commondale by J. Longstaff.
- 14 Cow and Calf Rocks, Ilkley by Bill Pates.
- 16 Dropping Well, Knaresborough (artist unknown).
- 23 Ripon Cathedral by Jim Gott.
- 29 Middleham Church by Maurice Healey.
- 33 Fountains Abbey (artist unknown).
- 35 Pickering Castle by B. R. Hammond.
- 41 Druid's Temple by D. A. Marsh.
- 44 Yorke's Folly, Guisecliffe by Stanley Bond.
- 47 Folly at Roseberry Topping by Bernard Fearnley.
- 49 Beggar's Bridge by Bernard Fearnley.
- 54 Dales food table (artist unknown).
- 60 Fairies in the garden (artist unknown).
- 63 The dreaded barguest (artist unknown).
- 64 Burnsall by Deborah Smart.
- 67 St. Gregory's Minster, Kirkdale by T. Armstrong.
- 69 Ainderby steeple by Stanley Bond.
- 77 Lead Church by Stanley Bond.
- 79 Richmond by Ruth Blackburn.